# The Dreams of the Gods

# The Dreams of the Gods

Poems by

J.R. Solonche

© 2023 J.R. Solonche. All rights reserved.
This material may not be reproduced in any form, published,
reprinted, recorded, performed, broadcast,
rewritten or redistributed without
the explicit permission of J.R. Solonche.
All such actions are strictly prohibited by law.

Cover design by Shay Culligan
Author photo credit by Emily Solonche

ISBN: 978-1-63980-339-2

Kelsay Books
502 South 1040 East, A-119
American Fork, Utah 84003
Kelsaybooks.com

# Books by J.R. Solonche

*Leda*
*The Book of a Small Fisherman*
*It's about Time*
*Around Here*
*The Lost Notebook of Zhao Li*
*Life-Size*
*Coming To*
*The Five Notebooks of Zhao Li*
*Selected Poems 2002—2021*
*Years Later*
*The Dust*
*A Guide of the Perplexed*
*The Moon Is the Capital of the World*
*For All I Know*
*The Time of Your Life*
*Enjoy Yourself*
*Piano Music*
*The Porch Poems*
*The Jewish Dancing Master*
*In a Public Place*
*If You Should See Me Walking on the Road*
*To Say the Least*
*True Enough*
*In Short Order*
*Tomorrow, Today, and Yesterday*
*Invisible*
*Won't Be Long*
*I, Emily Dickinson & Other Found Poems*
*Heart's Content*
*The Black Birch*
*Beautiful Day*
*Peach Girl: Poems for a Chinese Daughter* (with Joan I. Siegel)

# Contents

Part I

| | |
|---|---|
| The Dreams of the Gods | 15 |
| Silver | 16 |
| Wednesday | 17 |
| A Woods with Wings | 18 |
| Ambiguity | 19 |
| The Lake | 20 |
| The Clouds | 21 |
| The Nomination Is the Denomination of the Nation | 22 |
| The Nickel | 23 |
| The Ghost That Haunts the World Is Not Holy | 24 |
| Six of One | 25 |
| To My Tongue | 26 |
| When You've Seen One | 27 |
| Conversation | 28 |
| Easter | 29 |
| Goldfinches | 30 |
| Sonnet | 31 |
| After the Reading | 32 |
| The Best Myths Are the Metamorphoses | 33 |
| The Moon Is Still Mysterious | 34 |
| Medea Is the Message | 35 |
| The Lovers We Most Love Are the Tragic Lovers | 36 |
| With Apologies to Jonathan Swift | 37 |
| I Thought the Old Cherry | 38 |
| Swamp | 39 |
| It Looks Like | 40 |
| An Antique Torso of Apollo | 41 |
| Crossing | 42 |
| Fox | 43 |
| February Swamp | 44 |
| Blue | 45 |

Part II

Fifty Poems Based on First Lines
   by Emily Dickinson                                    49

Part III

| | |
|---|---|
| Dedication | 65 |
| We Were Talking About Zen | 66 |
| The Difference | 67 |
| A Place in the Woods | 68 |
| Assumption | 69 |
| I See | 70 |
| Sonnet | 71 |
| The Last Goldfinch Poem I Will Ever Write | 72 |
| Birch Tree | 73 |
| The Shadow | 74 |
| Sonnet | 75 |
| Among the Gods There Are No Tragedies | 76 |
| Bleeding Hearts | 77 |
| I Like the White Clouds Because They Transmute Gold to Silver | 78 |
| Distant Distances | 79 |
| Nursery Rhyme Rhyme Nursery | 80 |
| Sunflowers | 81 |
| Dark Clouds Come | 82 |
| Work | 83 |
| Without Apologies | 84 |
| Bar Talk | 85 |
| Perseus | 86 |
| Medusa | 87 |
| I Hear My Neighbor's Daughter | 88 |
| Memorial Day | 89 |
| Sonnet | 90 |

| | |
|---|---|
| If the Eye Could Write | 91 |
| I Want the Gods to Exist | 92 |
| Silverman | 93 |
| Double Windsor | 94 |
| There Are Three Things I Know for Sure | 95 |
| The White Peonies Explode | 96 |
| So Eve and Adam | 97 |
| Icarus | 98 |
| The Shield of Hector | 99 |

# Part I

# The Dreams of the Gods

Zeus dreams he's impotent.
Hera dreams she's single.
Hades dreams he's heaven-sent.
Iris that she's sitting still.

Athena dreams she's a dumb blonde.
Ares that his sword becomes a plowshare.
Nike dreams she finishes second.
Poseidon that he swims through air.

Apollo dreams he has stage fright.
Dionysus that he goes to AA.
Artemis dreams she slips out at night.
Hermes that he's lost his way.

Hephaestus dreams he's all thumbs.
Aphrodite dreams she finally cums.

# Silver

My favorite cowboy was *The Lone Ranger.*
His horse was named *Silver.*
His bullets were silver.
The actor who played Tonto was Jay Silverheels.
I hated Roy Rogers.
He sang.
The songs were stupid.
His horse was not white that looked silver.
His horse was a golden palomino.
I hated Gene Autry.
He sang.
The songs were stupid.
His horse was not white that looked silver.
I did like Hopalong Cassidy.
I liked his outfit.
It was black.
Even his hat was black.
He looked like a bad good guy.
Or a good bad guy.
He didn't sing.
His horse was named *Topper.*
It was white.
It looked silver.
I had a Hopalong Cassidy cap gun.
It wasn't silver.
It looked silver.
It shot caps that didn't shoot.
I knew they were silver, solid silver.

# Wednesday

One day is much like another.
But not that much.
Not so much that Wednesday is no longer Wednesday.
Wednesday is always Wednesday.
Wednesday is always the best day to wed.
Wednesday is always the best day to walk backward in the dew.
Wednesday mornings are always better than Wednesday nights.
Wednesday knights are never as adventuresome as Friday knights.
Friday knights always ride out on stallions of steel.
Wednesday knights always sleep in their armor.
Wednesday knights always dream of the beautiful damsel without mercy.
Friday knights always, always slay them.

# A Woods with Wings

A woods with wings,
the goldfinches swarm
the finch feeder, flutter,
scatter gold and black
like shadow-seeds,
like sun-seeds, all over.

# Ambiguity

When the wind
picked up,
it kicked up
all the leaves
raking up
missed in the fall,
but the rake
is stowed
away to stay
for spring's sake,
so the leaves
are free to go.

# The Lake

I live on a lake. Dave
owns six hundred acres
around the lake. He also
owns the lake. He recently
had a battle with the DEC.
Dave told me they wanted
him to fix the spillway.
They said it was out of
compliance. Dave disagreed.
He asked his lawyer about it.
His lawyer told him he didn't
have to obey the DEC. His
lawyer said Dave doesn't
own the lake. He said Dave
owns the ground but not
the water. So he doesn't
have to comply because it's
not his lake. That sounds like
a Zen koan, Dave, I said. No,
he said. It sounds like a headache.

# The Clouds

The clouds know all the grays,
display them one by one.
The sun doesn't stand a chance.
But the cherry stands its ground
to put its blossoms out,
sunlessly, cloudfully, all the same.

# The Nomination Is the Denomination of the Nation

I wanted to be worthy.
I wanted to be worth it.
I worried.
I worried much too much.
I was worried sick.
That worm squirmed in my belly.
That worm wriggled up and down.
That worm wagged its finger.
That worm wore me down to the bone.
That worm left me skin and bones.
That worthless worm.

# The Nickel

It should be two-faced.
It should not have a tail.
It should have the real tale.
It should show the two Jeffersons.
It should show the Declaration Jefferson.
It should show the slaver Jefferson.
The nickel should be two-faced like Jefferson.

# The Ghost That Haunts the World Is Not Holy

She is the ghost
of the earth we killed.

She is the ghost
of the earth we strangled in her sleep.

She is the ghost
of the earth who drank the poisoned cup we handed her.

She is the ghost
of the earth we wooed, won with our wickedness.

She is the ghost
of the earth we fooled, fouled with our folly.

The world is haunted by the ghost of the earth,
and she is not holy, not holy, not holy.

# Six of One

Although there's no more
happy fucking hour,
at least there's still
the fucking happy hour.

# To My Tongue

Good morning, tongue!
I see you there,
sticking out of my mouth
in the mirror,
leaning out of your window,
jabbing me in the chest
with your only finger.
What do you have to say for yourself?
Can you even speak by yourself?
Of course, you can't.
Of course, you can't speak by yourself.
You need the teeth.
You need the lips.
You need the larynx.
All you can do is mime.
All you can do is flap,
flop around like a fish out of water.
Too bad, tongue.
Say, *Aah,* O, la lingua!

# When You've Seen One

"A bald eagle just flew
over your house," I said
to my neighbor. "And
there are the other two,"
he said, pointing to a point
over my own house. "Wow,
I didn't see those," I said.
"Well, when you've seen
one, you've seen 'em all,"
he said, giving me a look,
you know the look I mean,
before turning back
to his yard work.

# Conversation

I am in the back.
The window opens.
It's my daughter.
"Why aren't you writing?" she says.
I look up from my notebook.
"What was that? I didn't hear you," I say.
"Why aren't you writing?" she says.
I look down at my notebook.
The page is still blank.
"Don't worry. I will. I just started," I said.
"Okay, but remember.
Don't come in until you do," she says.
"Okay, I'll remember," I say.
My daughter closes the window.
I won't tell her I'm cheating.

# Easter

Hey, Yeshua,
it's been two millennia
in heaven.
Come back, all is forgiven.

# Goldfinches

There were so many
at the feeder, I thought
the sun somehow was
responsible, so I asked
the sun if it was responsible,
and the sun beamed, *Yes*.

# Sonnet

The wind was blue with the sky.
The wind was gold with the sun.
The wind was white with the clouds.
The wind was black with the road.
The wind was green with the grass.
The wind was silver with the lake.
The wind was invisible with my mind.

The wind was jealous of the sky.
The wind was jealous of the sun.
The wind was jealous of the clouds.
The wind was jealous of the road.
The wind was jealous of the grass.
The wind was jealous of the lake.
The wind was not at all jealous of my mind.

## After the Reading

A woman came up to me.
"I like a lot of your poems,"
she said. "Thank you," I said.
"But I have to say that some
seem more like ghosts of poems
than real poems," she said.
"That's interesting," I said.
She walked away without
saying which was which.

# The Best Myths Are the Metamorphoses

The best myths
are the metamorphoses,
the ones that change,
transform, shift
shapes from one ordinary
to one more strange,
from one mere mortally
to one there immortally,
from a door to a portal,
from a casement to a window,
from a wife to a widow,
from a spoon to a knife,
from a moon-faced lover
to the lover of the moon.

# The Moon Is Still Mysterious

Regardless of the science,
the moon is still mysterious.
Regardless of the footprints on her face,
the moon is still mysterious.
Regardless of titanium's embrace,
the moon is still mysterious.

# Medea Is the Message

"Take that," she said.
"Take that and that and that," she said.
But that was not enough for her,
so she recorded it for us.
"Take this," she says.
"Take this and this and this," she says.
Forever.

# The Lovers We Most Love Are the Tragic Lovers

Tears and laughter do not come from the same place.
Tears come from a much deeper place than laughter.

We weep for Romeo and Juliet.
We weep for Pyramus and Thisbe.

We weep for Hero and Leander.
We weep for Tristan and Isolde.

We smile for Beatrice and Benedick.
We smile for Petruchio and Katherine.

We smile for Orsino and Viola.
We smile for Pat and Mike.

No, tears and laughter do not come from the same place.
Tears come from a much deeper well than laughter.

# With Apologies to Jonathan Swift

How beautiful in black and gold
Are the goldfinches to behold,
But when I need
To fill the feeder up with seed,
What's this stuff that looks like spit?
Oh! Goldfinches, Goldfinches, Goldfinches shit!

# I Thought the Old Cherry

I thought the old cherry
was dead there on the road's
shoulder, but it was not dead,
not yet, for today I saw one
branch in bloom, just one in bloom
over the road, all white,
all white like one arm in one sleeve
of its Sunday best, clean and pressed white shirt.

# Swamp

As I walked by
the swamp, two
of the three turtles
sunbathing on a log
sensed a threat so
jumped in while
the third stayed put,
somehow knowing
I was a poet.

# It Looks Like

It snowed so little,
how can I call it *snow*?
So I call it *oh, look,
it looks like it snowed.*
It is like the little way
you said you loved me.
I could not call it *love*,
so I called it *oh, look,
it looks a little like love.*
But that was years ago,
and look, what looked
like snow is gone already.

# An Antique Torso of Apollo

I cannot change my life. I've grown
too old, but if I could, I'd be a sculptor,
master of the chisel and hammer.
Then I would urge him from the stone
just like this. No need for centuries
to decapitate him and to lop off
his arms and legs and dick. He's enough.
There's plenty on the bone to seize
your gaze. Why wonder about what isn't there
when you can wander forth and back
admiring his back and front? Why dwell on lack
of head and limbs when you can stare
as you wish and be stared at, too,
by those nearby who only pretend they do?

# Crossing

Stopped at the railway crossing,
I cut the motor. It's the morning
freight, and I know I will be here
some time although I've never
counted the cars and do not now
as they file past me behind that
twinkling star-like light. They
duplicate themselves as a worm
does, adding segment to segment,
each one identically sized, identically
colored, identically shaped, clones
with different numbers only. I watch
them appear from the bend of trees,
I watch them pass the gates, I watch
them disappear into the bend of trees,
I close my eyes, I listen to them roll
over my thoughts, I listen to them roll
over my life, I listen to them roll until
the man behind me taps his horn.
"Give me a chance, friend," I say
into the mirror, "Give me a moment
to collect myself, for this train has rolled
over me and my ego. And then shall I
start up my engine. And then shall I cross
over and go on. I didn't see it was the end.
Mister, give me a moment to be born."

# Fox

I was on the phone
looking out the window.
Out of both corners
of my eye, I saw a big
red fox, the biggest
fox I've ever seen,
race across my lawn.
Its paws barely touched
the ground. Its tail
streamed behind,
a rocket's red exhaust.
I looked to see if it was
being chased. It wasn't.
I looked to see if it was
chasing something.
It wasn't. I don't know
why it was racing
across my lawn like
that, like a devil out
of hell. I don't know
why a devil would race
out of hell. I don't
remember who was
on the phone.

# February Swamp

It is frozen.
The sun is very bright.
The reflection of the sun
is very bright on the ice.
The two suns hurt my eyes.
I close them.
I stand still.

I listen for the dreams
of the turtles in the mud
at the bottom far below the ice.
I hear them, the dreams
which are all dreams
and are all the same dream.

# Blue

The sky was blue
so completely,
for a moment I thought
the world had forgotten
what clouds were,
but I wish it had been
longer than for only
a moment.

# Part II

# Fifty Poems Based on First Lines by Emily Dickinson

1.

*A counterfeit—a plated person.*
I sometimes think it's true
of me, not a genuine gentleman,
not sterling through and through.

2.

*A door just opened on a street,*
but no one came out.
Too bad. I was hoping to meet
someone to talk about.

3.

*A drunkard cannot meet a cork*
unless he heaves a great substantial sigh,
for it misses the bottle's mark
and means the contents have gone dry.

4.

*A feather from the whippowil*
I never found around these hills.
I've found a feather from the crow,
the owl, the jay, and the robin, though.

5.

*A nearness to tremendousness*
is not enough for me.
No, I the closer closest, the less
than atom space need be.


6.

*A thought went up my mind today,*
then down the other side.
It didn't last enough to stay
up there too long although it tried.


7.

*All but death can be adjusted.*
I'm not so sure of that,
for my life, entirely, it must be said,
has never changed, no matter what.


8.

*Better than music.*
Excuse me, Emily.
Here's the magic trick.
Nothing but your poetry.

9.

*By my window I have for scenery*
not so much. There's a pink magnolia.
There's a white wild cherry.
Never mind. It's spring! Ah!


10.

*Circumference thou bride of awe.*
Ravished? Or unravished like the urn?
The strangest bridegrooms I ever saw,
his *quietness* and your *awe*. I'm concerned.


11.

*Drama's vitallest expression is the common day.*
I really don't know what to say.
But this is nothing new.
Hey, look. The sky is blue.


12.

*I've got an arrow here*
and here and here and here.
A Cupid army must be out there
to know the target best to share.

13.

*Each life converges to some centre,*
as yours converged to house, to room,
to window, to worn pine floor,
to paper, to thread, to needle, to poem.


14.

*Go not too near a house of rose.*
I tried it once. I rang the bell.
A lady opened the door. Her nose
was hairy. She was fat and smelled like hell.


15.

*My reward for being was this:*
I was given a life of average years,
granted both a poet's and a widow's kiss,
and my fair share—no, much more!—of tears.


16.

*Over the fence*
I hear my neighbor's noise,
his party of gas powered instruments,
his smoke spewing, wood chewing toys.

17.

*Sweet is the swamp with its secrets.*
The turtle's repose on the log,
the heron's balance, the egret's
eye, the bull horn of the bull frog.


18.

*Your thought don't have words everyday*
although it seems they do for you.
I'm happy that mine have something to say
whenever the hell they do.


19.

*Why should we hurry—why indeed?*
Let us banish hurry from the world,
unflight the winged aluminum steed.
May the flag of sweet *Slowness* be unfurled.


20.

*Which is the best—the moon or the crescent?*
My answer is neither one.
The best is night with no moon lent
for any light at all. No, none.

21.

*Not with a club the heart is broken,*
not with a spade the diamond
blunted and beaten down.
Of course, it all depends upon the game at hand.


22.

*Not at home to callers,*
I am at home, but not seem
to them, the telemarketers,
the answerer's my answering machine.


23.

*I'll clutch and clutch,*
I'll rev and rev,
but I'll never get much
good at driving this old Chev.


24.

*The definition of beauty is*
"the quality or aggregate of qualities
in a person or thing that gives pleasure
to the senses or exalts the mind or spirit."(Merriam-Webster)

25.

*My eye is fuller than my vase.*
My eye one tulip in it has
while the other an empty space.
Or did she pronoun it *vase*?


26.

*There is a finished feeling*
in the air today,
like a wound is healing,
like the heel of health holds its way.


27.

*This was a poet,*
but they didn't know it
because you didn't show it.
Emily, why did you blow it?


28.

*You know that portrait in the moon,*
you know the one I'm speaking of,
the one men made, that rune
of boots that ruined the cheek I love?

29.

*Time does go on*
so there's just no stopping it.
On and on, Time's never done
with all sorts of shit.


30.

*You'll find it when you try to die.*
No, I don't think I'll ever try dying.
It seems as impossible as to fly,
yet for that, I could very well die trying.


31.

*It sounded as if the streets were running,*
but they weren't, I admit.
The silence out there was stunning.
My mind and I and commotion didn't fit.


32.

*We never know we go when we are going.*
It's only after, long after, we arrive
that we finally know we were knowing.
For many this might be known as being alive.

33.

*We dream—it is good we are dreaming,*
for the mind must mend the tears
that the day delivers teeming
with troubles, with carts full of cares.


34.

*To wait an hour is long,*
no matter what you wait for,
for that one to come along,
for that word, for that door.


35.

*One and one are one.*
Two and two are two.
Three and three are fun.
Four and four are you.


36.

*Within my reach*
there is all I need,
not all I want. So teach
me, please, all about greed.

37.

*Meeting by accident,*
I kissed the widow Taylor.
I kissed her twice, then went
behind her trailer.


38.

*An everywhere of silver.*
That's the everywhere I want to make.
A silver everything, down to the sliver
and the splinter, and all for ungold's sake.


39.

*At last to be identified,*
I send them here and there,
knowing most shall be denied
a welcome for what they wear.


40.

*To make routine a stimulus*
is a skill I've learned quite well.
Now it's become my little lust,
my daily dutiful day in hell.

41.

*How far is it to heaven?*
I know you wrote it with a capital.
My heaven is unleavened,
a Hebrew heaven with "h" in small.


42.

*The road was lit with moon and star.*
It was quiet all around the lake.
Then, suddenly, a car
came with noisy horn and noisier brake.


43.

*There is a word*
that you will never see,
one that you've never heard,
or ever will, or read, or think, or be.


44.

*The heart is the capital of the mind.*
It's where the government resides.
It's where you'll find
the makers of the Law take their shifting sides.

45.

*The clouds their backs together laid.*
Perhaps they'll turn over now to show
a missionary zeal, and unafraid,
a public display of cumulonimbus porno.


46.

*Hope is a strange invention.*
Never patented by the inventor,
who, so altruistic in intention,
gave it free to us, our other air.


47.

*It was a quiet seeming day.*
At least it was 'til three.
Then the kids came home to play
and their old man cut down a tree.


48.

*So the eyes accost and sunder.*
So the ears scent sound.
So the nostril is all wonder.
So the tongue squares words to round.

49.

*Let us play yesterday.*
It's Paul McCartney's greatest tune.
I'm in a melancholy way,
but I'll be better soon.


50.

*Within my reach*
are all I require:
pen, paper, peach
schnapps, weed, fire.

# Part III

# Dedication

I want what he got,
what Hippolytus
got, not the life, not
the death, but after
that godawful mess,
the way the maidens,
before they married,
cut off a lock of hair
for him in dedication
with such tenderness.

# We Were Talking About Zen

We were talking about Zen.
"So, Jim," I said. "When
a tree falls in the forest
and there's no one around
to hear it, does it make a sound?"
"No, it doesn't make a sound,
it makes a lot of sounds,"
Jim said. "What do you mean?"
I said. "It makes one sound
to a squirrel, another to a raccoon,
another to a toad, another to a crow,
to a possum, to a bear, and so on
and so forth. Get it?" "I think so,"
I said. "I hadn't thought of that."
"Neither to the guy who came
up with that koan," said Jim.

# The Difference

I have not lost
my mind.

I have loosed
my mind.

You will find
there's a difference.

One or the other
will make sense.

One of the other
will be the ghost.

# A Place in the Woods

My daughter bought a 1000-piece
jigsaw puzzle to keep her busy while
staying at home. It's called *A Place
in the Woods*. (I consulted the Modern
Language Association style manual
for how to format the name of a jigsaw
puzzle, but they didn't provide one,
so I did it in italics.) It's very bucolic.
There's a cottage by a stream, a wooden
bridge over the stream, a happy pair
of swans gliding down the stream,
a canoe on the bank, a family of deer
drinking from the stream, two cardinals
in a tree above the stream, a robin flying.
There are two Adirondack chairs, one green,
one red, a well for water or a wishing well
(which one is really impossible to tell)
and there are flowers, flowers, flowers,
flowers by the hundreds all over the place,
tulips, pansies, hyacinths, daffodils,
and lots whose names I do not know.
It must be springtime, or summer,
but there is also snow. Snow is everywhere.
And icicles. Can you believe it? Icicles.
Spring flowers, summer flowers, winter snow
and icicles. It's Eden in every season but fall.
It's Paradise before the Fall. It's a puzzle.

# Assumption

A precocious
bumble bee has
stumbled here
from somewhere,
and finding the garden
bare of bloom,
so stumbles on elsewhere,
one must assume.

# I See

I see the goldfinches
in the beech tree
behind me.
Quite a colony.
Good for you, sorry
old beech tree.
Good for you, tree
I now envy.

# Sonnet

You should have known what it meant.
You should have seen it coming.
You should not have been so content.
You should have heeded the humming.

You should never have been so slow.
You should have been prepared and ready.
You should have known full well to know.
You should have been sure and steady.

You should have read it in their faces.
You should have seen their cheeks were flushed.
You should have heard it in their voices.
You should have felt shoved when they pushed.

You should have sensed their voices trembled.
You should have asked, "For what are you assembled?"

# The Last Goldfinch Poem I Will Ever Write

How much blacker
and golder
the males are,
but how
much by far
are the females bolder.

# Birch Tree

In the woods, there is
a solitary birch tree
which has become special
to me. I visit it regularly.
I brought my jackknife
once to carve my name
into its white bark. Or
maybe a haiku. I almost
did, but I stopped short.
I couldn't bring myself
to bring the blade to touch
the trunk. This is the haiku
I wanted to write:

*Among all these trees,*
*I am the only white one.*
*Ah. No. Not lonely.*

# The Shadow

The shadow
of a hawk
passed through
my shadow
as I walked
around the lake.
One day it will take
my shadow with it
to its high place
that I will never find.

# Sonnet

The morning wakes up gagging on green.
The sky spits out the sun.
The sun drools down the sky's blue chin.
One white cloud, one gray cloud post their banns.
My shadow coincides my noon.
Inside out, my shadow becomes my soul again.
Outside in, my shadow as my soul is done.
Already after noon it is afternoon.
I will hear the gallop of my neighbor's Mustang soon.
The sun sets in the horizon's frown.
There is no night, for now is the day of the moon.
It says, "Settle down, settle down."
The stars chime in, "Settle down, settle down."
The dream wakes up and is gone. *(What an awful line.)*

# Among the Gods There Are No Tragedies

Among the gods, there are no tragedies.
The greatest pain is insulted vanity,
the greatest suffering is jealousy.
They do what they please
without ever saying, "Please."
Whomever they want they seize
by force or trickery
or seduce with the beauty of a swan.
But listen,
any mortal who plays his cards right,
may be beloved
of a god.
And then himself become a god.
Thereafter a starry constellation every night.
Not bad.

# Bleeding Hearts

On the phone,
96-year-old Eva says it's too early
for bleeding hearts to bloom.
On the phone,
I am looking at mine bloom
in the garden,
but I don't have the heart to tell her.

# I Like the White Clouds Because They Transmute Gold to Silver

I like the white clouds.
The white clouds transmute gold to silver.

I do not like gold.
I love silver.

My first memory of silver is a dollar of silver.
It was my father's silver dollar.

He gave it to me to strike the fire engine's bell.
The bell was not of silver.

It looked like silver.
It made the sound of silver.

I love anything that looks like silver.
I loved the silver hair of my grandmother.

I did not like the gold hair of my cousin.
I love anything that can tarnish like silver.

I love anything that can be polished like silver.
I do not like gold.

Gold does not tarnish.
Gold is incorruptible.

Gold is the saint of metals.
I do not like saints

# Distant Distances

There is distance and there are distances.
These could be the same.
These could be different.
There are distant relatives.
There are close relatives.
These could be the same.
Most know how to keep their distance.
Then there is that one with that distant look on her face.
This one is not to be confused with that one
with that faraway look in her eye.
The eye and the face are different.

# Nursery Rhyme Rhyme Nursery

This is their room.
This is moon's and spoon's room.
This is Jill's and hill's room.
This is down's and crown's room.
This is water's and after's room.
This is Muffet's and tuffet's room.
This is wall's and fall's room.
This is Peep's and sheep's room.
This is snow's and go's room.
This is Sprat's and fat's room.
This is Horner's and corner's room.
This is thumb's and plum's room.
This is dock's and clock's room.
This is treacle's and weasel's room.
This is rye's and pie's room.
This is sing's and king's room.
This is womb's and tomb's and gloom's
and doom's room.

# Sunflowers

Sunflowers always face the sun.
I have seen them, so I know.
When there is no sun, sunflowers face each other.
I have not seen them, but I've heard this is true.
I believe it.
I would believe anything sunflowers do.

# Dark Clouds Come

Dark clouds come
between the trees and the sun.
The dark clouds say,
"You have had enough sun for one day.
You need the rain now.
And that is where we come in."
The trees have heard all this before.
They tolerate the pomposity of the dark clouds.
The sun, however, is visibly annoyed.
It silently burns behind their backs.

# Work

I was sweeping the walk
with an old straw broom.
Emily stuck her head out
the window. "In Disney
movies, when the girl
sweeps like that the birds
sing," she said. "Listen,"
I said. "The birds are singing."
"But in the movies, the birds
help the girl sweep," she said.
"Well, this is not a Disney
movie," I said. "And you are
not a girl," she said and
closed the window.

# Without Apologies

I have a wheelbarrow.
It isn't red.
Not much depends upon it.
I don't have chickens.
My neighbor has chickens.
They make a mess of my mulch.
They shit like crazy on my walk.
I wish it would rain.

# Bar Talk

"I'd give anything
for the love of one
good woman," he said.
"Or one good woman
and two bad ones,"
said the other.

# Perseus

I almost peeked. How could it be true?
No one could be that horridly ugly.
No one could possibly be that ghastly.
Turn men into stone? Turn boys into stone, yes.
Any old hag could do that. I've witnessed it many times.
My own grandmother turned me into stone once.
But to turn a man into stone?
A man who has slept with hundreds of women?
Young, old, fair, swarthy, slender, fat?
A man who has been everywhere, seen everything?
No. I did not believe it. But I brought my shield anyway.
Just in case. As insurance. And as I say, I almost looked at her.
I felt pity. For a moment, I truly pitied her.
I even wanted to tenderly touch her face.
I wanted to whisper, "I'm sorry." And I did.
I did whisper to her. As I looked in my shield
and slew her, I whispered, "Forgive me."

# Medusa

So you think you're a hero, do you?
A big man. What a fool you are.
I used you. I wanted to die.
I wanted you to kill me.
I was tired of turning men to stone.
I no longer got any satisfaction from it.
It was too easy. I could do it in my sleep.
Do you really think you could fool me?
I knew what you were up to. I let you do it.
Your sword was sharp. You were fast.
Thank you for that, at least. Your lips moved.
Did you whisper something? I didn't hear.
Some hero. Some man. You looked like
a fairy with those stupid wings on your shoes.
That's right. I saw them.
That magical cap wasn't so magical.

# I Hear My Neighbor's Daughter

I hear my neighbor's daughter.
She says, "Dad."
I remember my neighbor when he was a kid.
I heard him say, "Dad."
His dad said, "What?"
He says, "What?"
The rest is unimportant.
It is not meant to be remembered.

# Memorial Day

What happened to his uniform?
I never saw it.
She must not have kept it.
A shame.
She should have kept it.
But she kept the cap.
I remember it.
I remember putting it on.
It was too big.
I remember it was olive drab.
I remember it was soft felt.
I remember the brass insignia.
It was an eagle.
I don't know what happened to it.
She didn't keep it.
I should have kept it.
I should be looking at it now in front of me,
still too big.

# Sonnet

There was always another place.
That was where I wanted to be.
There was always another time.
That was when I wanted to be.
There was always another face.
That was the face I wanted to see.
There was always another voice.
That was the one I wanted to hear.
There was always another road.
That was the one I wanted to travel.
There was always another hand.
That was the one I wanted to hold.
There was always one named *Another.*
That was always the one I wanted.

# If the Eye Could Write

If the eye could write,
it would tell exactly what it sees.

If the lips could see,
they would swear them all to secrecy.

# I Want the Gods to Exist

I want the gods to exist.
I want them to exist for just one day.
One hour will be enough.
I want to insult one to her face.
I want to insult her so she could turn me
into something.
Turn me into a tree, or a flower, or a bird,
or best of all, a rock.
A rock on the coastline of an island in
the Mediterranean Sea.
A rock famous for its shape of a man
with a mysterious smile on his face.

# Silverman

Silverman was not a silver man.
Silverman was a silver woman.
She wanted to mine gold.
Instead she mined silver.
She wanted to be quick.
Instead she was slow.
She was here.
She was there.
She was everywhere.
Then she was gone, reputedly tarnished.

# Double Windsor

I learned how to tie a double
Windsor knot from my father.
The double Windsor was more
complex than the half Windsor.
It required more overs and unders.
I practiced it over and over
until I mastered it. I learned
it by heart as all things worth
learning are learned. I learned
it for his funeral. And for hers.
Who will tie it at mine? I wonder.

# There Are Three Things I Know for Sure

There are three things I know for sure.
I know I am free to do anything I wish.
I know I am not free to do anything I wish.
I know this is not ironic.

# The White Peonies Explode

The white peonies explode.
"Why are you so angry?" I ask.
"We are not angry," they answer.
"We cannot contain our sexual energy."
"But you are almost as old as I am," I say.
"When I explode nowadays, it is from anger."
"We are flowers," say the white peonies.
"Be thankful that you are flowers and not men," I say.
"O, we are, we assure you, we are," say the white peonies.

# So Eve and Adam

So Eve and Adam ate
from the wrong tree.
That apple brought them death.
They should have eaten
from the Tree of Life.
Maybe they did.
Who knows?
But the serpent knew.
That's why he chose the Knowledge Tree.
And what exactly did he get out of it?
The loss of limbs and the enmity of man
in exchange for the satisfaction
of fucking up Eden and dissing god
with eternal hissing?
Not bad.

# Icarus

Did you ever wonder who the mother of Icarus was?
Did you ever wonder if he had an Oedipus complex?
We know nothing whatsoever
of the wife of Daedalus, Icarus's mother.
Who the hell was she?
Do you think she would have allowed
her only son to do that dumb thing he did,
fly so close to the sun
with those idiotic waxen wings?
Of course, she isn't in the story.
There would be no story if she were.
It's the same with *Lear.*
Shakespeare knew what he was doing.
It never fails.
The wives, the mothers, are never around
when you need them most.
Had Lear's wife been there to stop the nonsense,
forget the whole thing.
No tragedy today, ladies and gentlemen.
No eyes gouged out.
No hangings.
No beautiful golden boy drowning in the sea.

# The Shield of Hector

The shield of Hector
was not much to see,
just bronze and leather,
so unlike that of Achilles,
the great masterpiece
Hephaestus made,
but Hector's stained shield
smelled of the sweat he shed
in battle, and was used to carry
his son, Astyanax, dead
from Troy and was the coffin
he was buried in.

## About the Author

Nominated for the National Book Award and nominated three times for the Pulitzer Prize, J.R. Solonche is the author of 33 books of poetry and coauthor of another. He lives in the Hudson Valley.

www.ingramcontent.com/pod-product-compliance
Lightning Source LLC
Chambersburg PA
CBHW030053170426
43197CB00010B/1509